# TREES, WEEDS, AND VEGETABLES— SO MANY KINDS OF PLANTS!

## Mary Dodson Wade

*Series Science Consultant:*
**Mary Poulson, Ph.D.**
Associate Professor of Plant Biology
Department of Biological Sciences
Central Washington University
Ellensburg, WA

*Series Literacy Consultant:*
**Allan A. De Fina, Ph.D.**
Past President of the New Jersey Reading Association
Chairperson, Department of Literacy Education
New Jersey City University
Jersey City, NJ

# CONTENTS

# WORDS TO KNOW

**bulbs (BULBZ)**—A fat, underground part of some plants. Bulbs store food for the plant.

**evergreen (EH vur green)**— A plant that stays green all year.

**spores (SPORZ)**—Tiny bits of a plant that make new plants.

**vegetable (VEJ tuh bul)**— The part of a plant that people can eat.

**woody**—Plants with hard stems, such as trees and bushes.

## PARTS OF A PLANT

flower

leaf

stem

roots

# MANY KINDS OF
# PLANTS

There are about 350,000 different kinds of plants in the world! Some plants are big, and some are small. Some have hard wood, and others do not. Some plants stay green all year, and others lose their leaves each fall.

# TREES AND BUSHES

Trees and bushes have stiff stems and branches. They are called **woody** plants. They can have many branches. Some are very tall, such as oak trees. Others may be shorter than you are, such as rose bushes.

This tree's leaves change color in the fall. Then the leaves drop to the ground.

# LEAVES THAT STAY GREEN AND LEAVES THAT FALL

Some trees and bushes stay green all year. They are called **evergreens**. Other plants lose their leaves every year. The leaves drop to the ground in the fall. The tree or bush grows new leaves in the spring.

**Pine trees are evergreens. Their leaves are called needles.**

# GRASSES

Grasses have long, soft leaves. Different kinds of grasses grow all over the world. Wheat, marsh grass, and bamboo are grasses. Some kinds of green grasses grow on lawns and in parks.

Grass flowers are not very bright or colorful. Instead, they can be brown and fluffy or spiky.

grass flower

# WILDFLOWERS

Wildflowers usually grow with grasses. They are called "wild" flowers because they were not planted by a person. Many wildflowers are bright and colorful. They grow in fields and next to the road.

Queen Anne's Lace is a kind of wildflower.

Some people
like dandelions.
Do you?

# WEEDS

Weeds are any plants that grow where they are not wanted. They take water and space away from other plants. Dandelion weeds have pretty flowers, but most people do not want these weeds. They only want grass to grow.

# VEGETABLES
## AND FRUITS

**Vegetables** are the parts of plants that people can eat. Different vegetables come from different parts of the plant.

Broccoli is a bunch of flowers, and lettuce is leaves.

lettuce

broccoli

carrots

garlic

Carrots are roots,
and garlic is a **bulb**.

Fruit is part of
a plant, too.
Strawberries
are fruit, and so
are tomatoes.

strawberries

Many ferns grow on this forest floor.

# MOSSES
## AND FERNS

Mosses are small soft plants that grow in clumps. Ferns have long green leaves with pretty patterns.

moss

# DIFFERENT WAYS TO MAKE NEW PLANTS

Most plants make flowers. The flowers make seeds. The seeds grow into new plants.

**This seed is starting to grow.**

Other plants grow each year from plant parts under the ground. Beach grass grows from special roots. Tulips grow from bulbs.

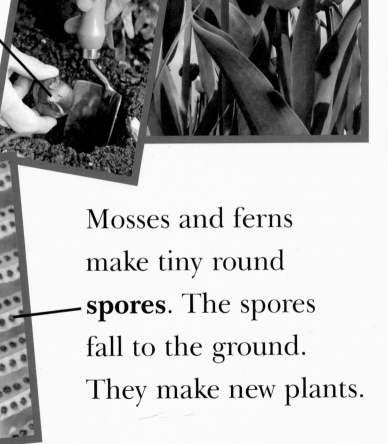

Mosses and ferns make tiny round **spores**. The spores fall to the ground. They make new plants.

21

# WHICH PLANTS LIVE
# NEAR YOU?

> **You will need:**
> * a piece of paper
> * crayons or colored pencils

1. Use brown and dark green to draw the woody plants (trees and bushes) in your yard or local park.

2. Use other colors to draw plants that are not woody (flowers and grasses). Does your yard have more woody plants or plants that are not woody?

# LEARN MORE

## BOOKS

Gibbons, Gail. *Tell Me, Tree: All About Trees for Kids*. Boston: Little Brown & Co., 2002.

Jenkins, Martin. *Fly Traps!: Plants That Bite Back*. New York: Walker Books, Ltd., 2001.

Loves, June. *Ferns*. Philadelphia: Chelsea Clubhouse, 2005.

Stewart, Melissa. *A Parade of Plants*. Minneapolis: Compass Point Books, 2004.

## WEB SITES

**University of Illinois. *The Great Plant Escape.*** <http://www.urbanext.uiuc.edu/gpe>

**U.S. Department of Agriculture. *Sci4Kids*. "Plants."** <http://www.ars.usda.gov/is/kids/plants/plantsintro.htm>

# INDEX

Enslow Elementary, an imprint of Enslow Publishers, Inc.
Enslow Elementary® is a registered trademark of
Enslow Publishers, Inc.

**Library of Congress Cataloging-in-Publication Data**

Wade, Mary Dodson.
  Trees, weeds, and vegetables—so many kinds of plants! /
    Mary Dodson Wade.
    p. cm. — (I like plants!)
    Summary: "Presents information about different types of
      plants" Provided by publisher.
    Includes bibliographical references and index.
    ISBN-13: 978-0-7660-3156-2 (library ed.)
    ISBN-10: 0-7660-3156-X (library ed.)
    1. Plants—Juvenile literature. I. Title.
    QK49.W115 2009
    580—dc22                   2007039460

ISBN-13: 978-0-7660-3616-1 (paperback)
ISBN-10: 0-7660-3616-2 (paperback)

Printed in the United States of America

10 9 8 7 6 5 4 3 2 1

Every effort has been made to locate all copyright holders of
material used in this book. If any errors or omissions have
occurred, corrections will be made in future editions of this book.

**To Our Readers:** We have done our best to make sure all
Internet Addresses in this book were active and appropriate
when we went to press. However, the author and the publisher
have no control over and assume no liability for the material
available on those Internet sites or on other Web sites they may
link to. Any comments or suggestions can be sent by e-mail to
comments@enslow.com or to the address on the back cover.

♻ Enslow Publishers, Inc., is committed to printing our books on
recycled paper. The paper in every book contains 10% to 30% post-
consumer waste (PCW). The cover board on the outside of each book
contains 100% PCW. Our goal is to do our part to help young people and the environment too!

**Note to Parents and Teachers:** The *I Like Plants!* series supports the
National Science Education Standards for K–4 science. The Words to
Know section introduces subject-specific vocabulary words, including
pronunciation and definitions. Early readers may need help with
these new words.

**Photo Credits:** © 2008 Jupiterimages Corporation, pp. 18, 21
(fern); © Avril O'Reilly/Alamy, p. 15; Bob Gibbons/Photo
Researchers, Inc., pp. 1, 12; iStockphoto.com: © Cornelia Pithart,
p. 17 (garlic), © Malcolm Romain, p. 3; Michael P. Gadomski/Photo
Researchers, Inc., p. 11; Nicole diMella, p. 19; © Peter Griffith/
Masterfile, p. 10; Shutterstock, pp. 2, 4, 8, 9, 14, 16 (lettuce), 21
(tulips); UpperCut/Punchstock, p. 7; Visuals Unlimited: © Dick Poe,
p. 13, © FhF Greenmedia/Gap Photo, p. 21 (bulb), © Inga Spence,
pp. 16 (broccoli), 17 (strawberries), © J S Sira/Gap Photo, p. 6,
© Nigel Cattlin, pp. 17 (carrots), 20.

**Cover Photo:** Shutterstock

**Enslow Elementary**
an imprint of
**Enslow Publishers, Inc.**
40 Industrial Road
Box 398
Berkeley Heights, NJ 07922
USA
    http://www.enslow.com